Multi-Cooker Made Simple...

Paul Brodel & Dee Hunwicks

Introduction

The Multi-Cooker is an invaluable item in the kitchen. Why ? The answer is simple; it does exactly what it says on the box. It multi cooks, it's quick, enables you to make anything from a snack to family meals to a special dinner party treat.

It's a one-stop shop for your cooking needs with a huge capacity, heat control and easy quick clean up.

You will see as you thumb through the pages, the recipes are simple, easy to follow and the majority can be made with store cupboard and freezer ingredients. However, there are also lots of special dishes that we really hope tickle your taste buds!

There are plenty of handy hints if you want to change some of the recipes yourself.

Enjoy and happy cooking!

CONTENTS / INDEX

Starters / Appetizers:

PAGE

  7 Buttery Crab
  9 Cauliflower Soup
 11 Cheese Fondue
 13 Frittata
 15 Mozzarella & Sun-dried Tomato Risotto with Butternut Squash
 17 Naan Bread
 19 Pea and Ham Risotto
 21 Red Lentil Soup
 23 Salmon Pâté with Dill and Mustard Sauce
 25 Toasted Sandwich
 27 Tomato and Basil Bruschetta
 29 Wild Mushroom and Bacon Risotto

Main Courses / Entrée:

 31 Beef Bourguignon
 33 Beef Stew and Dumplings
 35 Calzone
 37 Chicken Tikka Masala
 39 Chilli Beef Stir Fry
 41 Chilli Con Carne with Tortillas and Mexican Chilli Cheese Dip
 43 Dough Balls / Cornbread / Corn Dogs
 45 Duck in Orange Sauce
 47 Gnocchi with Gorgonzola Spinach and Pine Nuts
 49 Kedgeree
 51 Lamb Burgers
 53 Lemon Chicken
 55 Mexican Style Rice
 57 Paella
 59 Pasta with Ham and Parmesan
 61 Poached Trout with Herb Stuffing

Main Courses / Entrée: (Continued)

PAGE

63 Pork Chops with Spicy Tomato Sauce and Stir-fry Cabbage
65 Pork Steaks with Wine and Apple Sauce
67 Quick Cheese Pasta
69 Red Thai Curry with Prawns and Aubergine
71 Rosti Brunch
73 Sausage with Onion Gravy
75 Southern Fried Chicken
77 Spanish Omelette
79 Special Fried Rice
81 Spicy Sausage Casserole
83 Steak with a Pepper Sauce
85 Teriyaki Prawns with Vegetable Stir Fry
87 Tomato and Mince Pasta Bake
89 Tuna Pasta
91 Veggie Burger

Desserts:

93 Apple Crumble
95 Banana Cake with Chocolate Caramel
97 Chocolate Croissant Pudding
99 Chocolate Orange Puddings
101 Crêpe Suzette
103 Dropped Scones
105 Raspberry & Coconut Pudding
107 Rice Pudding with Apricots
109 Spicy Prunes
111 Syrup Pudding
113 Winter Warming Fruit Salad

Handy Hints

114 Cooking Tips
115 Measurement Guide

Buttery Crab

Ingredients
2 tins white crab meat
1 tin anchovy fillets (optional)
1 medium glass white wine
50g (2 oz) white breadcrumbs
50g (2 oz) butter
25g (1 oz) chopped parsley
(12g or ½ oz if using dried)
25g (1 oz) chopped fresh dill
(12g or ½ oz if using dried)
Juice ½ lemon
A pinch of nutmeg
Pepper
Garnish
Lemon wedges, cooked prawns
and rocket.
     Serves 4

Method
1. Turn the Multi-Cooker to number 1, add in all the ingredients, white crab meat, prawns, anchovies, white wine, white breadcrumbs, butter, chopped dill, chopped parsley, lemon juice, nutmeg, when adding the anchovies, no further salt is required.
2. Cook out for seven minutes, stirring constantly, season with white pepper.

Handy Hint
A wonderful starter that you can serve with hot toast or melba toast (simply make normal toast then remove the crusts, cut the toast into two slices so that it is cooked on one side and uncooked on the other).
This recipe also makes a tasty meal for lunch or supper.

7

Cauliflower Soup

Ingredients
1 medium cauliflower (broken into florets)
2 medium onions (finely chopped)
285ml (1 pint) Milk
1 litre (1 ¾ pints) chicken or vegetable stock
Pinch granulated sugar
1 large potato (peeled and cubed)
1 tbsp olive oil
125ml (¼ pint) double cream
½ tsp ground cumin
1 tbsp chopped parsley
1 tbsp butter
A pinch of mixed herbs
Salt and pepper
Garnish
1 tbsp chopped parsley
        Serves 4

Method
1. Heat the oil in the Multi-Cooker pan for 1 minute at number 3 and fry the onions for 2 minutes.
2. Add the cauliflower florets, potato, mixed herbs, cumin, butter and keep stirring for 3 minutes.
3. Add chicken or vegetable stock with the sugar and bring to the boil on number 5, with the lid on.
4. Turn the heat down to number 1 to simmer. Put a spoon between the pan and the lid to reduce lid rattle, note that the spoon handle may be hot, so wear gloves/mitts; cook for 15 minutes stirring every 5 minutes.
5. Add the milk and cream, bring to the boil for 3 minutes on number 4.
6. Turn off the Multi-Cooker, allow to cool for 5 minutes then pour or ladle the soup into a blender. Blend to a fine consistency and season to taste. Always take care to follow the manufacturer's instructions when blending hot liquids.

Serve with crusty bread and butter.

Cheese Fondue

Ingredients
1 French stick cut into cubes
1 clove of garlic
500ml (16 fluid oz) white wine
200g (8 oz) Emmental (grated)
200g 8 oz Gruyère (grated)
2 tbsp corn flour
Serve with
Carrot, celery, bread and grapes
Serves 6

Method

1. Rub the garlic clove around the inside of the Multi-Cooker pan.
2. Add the wine and warm on number 3, slowly mixing in the cheeses with a plastic whisk or wooden spoon. Stir continuously until you have added all the cheese and it is thoroughly mixed.
3. Mix the corn flour with a little water and pour into the Multi-Cooker, stirring continuously .
4. Bring to the boil then turn down to just under number 1 to keep warm.
5. Serve with cubed bread, celery sticks, carrot sticks and grapes. Use wooden skewers to avoid scratching the non-stick coating.

Frittata

Ingredients
4 large baking potatoes (peeled and cubed)
2 tbsp olive oil
1 red onion (finely chopped)
1 tsp garlic paste
1 yellow pepper (diced)
1 courgette (diced)
100g (4oz) peas
9 medium eggs
50g (2oz) Gruyère cheese (grated)
2 tbsp chopped fresh parsley
(or 1 tbsp of dried)
Salt & pepper (pinch)
Garnish
Tomatoes
Lettuce
Salad dressing
Serves 6

Method
1. Put 1 litre (1¾ pints) of boiling water into the Multi-Cooker and turn on to number 3½. Add potatoes and boil for 5 minutes with the lid on.
2. Drain excess water off potatoes and remove from the Multi-Cooker.
3. Add oil to the Multi-Cooker pan and fry onions, garlic, courgette, peas and peppers at number 3½ for 3 minutes without burning them. Add potatoes and fry them for 2 minutes on number 2.
4. Beat the eggs and mix in the cheese, parsley, salt & pepper in a bowl, pour over the fried vegetables and potatoes in the Multi-Cooker.
5. Turn down Multi-Cooker to just under number 1 (so the thermostat light comes on / off) and cook out, with the lid on for 12 minutes or until thoroughly cooked, being careful not to let it burn.
6. Using a plastic spatula cut into desired portions and turn over to show browned underside on the plate.

13

Mozzarella and Sun-dried Tomato Risotto with Butternut Squash

Ingredients
250g (10 oz) Arborio rice
1 large onion (chopped)
1 tsp mixed dried herbs
1 tbsp olive oil
150g (6 oz) mozzarella (cubed)
150g (6 oz) sundried tomatoes in olive oil
50g (2 oz) tomato puree
50g (2 oz) parmesan cheese (grated)
1.1 litre (1¾ pints) chicken stock
125mls (¼ pint) white wine
200g (8 oz) cream cheese
Salt and pepper

Garnish
75g (3 oz) grated parmesan
Basil leaves

Serve with
Tomato, red onion and green leaf salad

Serves 6

Method
1. Add the onions and oil to Multi-Cooker and fry for 3 minutes on number 4.
2. Add the risotto rice and cook out for 2 minutes stirring continuously.
3. Add the tomato puree and stir.
4. Add the white wine, stock, butternut squash, mixed herbs and sundried tomatoes slowly stirring every 2 minutes with the lid on at number 2 for 12 minutes.
5. Add the cream cheese, mozzarella and parmesan, gently mixing in for 3 minutes. Season to taste. Garnish with basil leaves.
6. Serve with tomatoes, onion, and green leaf salad with balsamic glaze.

15

Naan Bread

Ingredients
1 tsp sugar
1 tsp dried yeast
200g (8 oz) plain flour
1 tsp salt
1 tsp baking powder
1 tbsp vegetable oil
2 tbsp plain yogurt
2 tbsp warm milk
¼ tsp black onion seeds
3 tbsp warm water
Garnish
mango chutney
tomato & onion salad with cumin seeds
sour cream mixed with mint sauce
        Serves 5

Method

1.Mix the yeast with warm milk, water and sugar, leave for 4 minutes until the yeast is covered with froth.
2.Mix together the flour, onion seeds, salt, baking powder, oil and yogurt then stir into the yeast mixture.
3.Knead the mixture for 5 minutes. Alternatively you could use a food mixer with a dough hook, adding more flour if necessary.
4.Flour your hands and separate small pieces of the dough to make 5 small individual naan breads.
5.Roll into balls, then spread out with your hands to the size you require (approximately 7mm or ¼ inch thick).
6.Place a dusting of flour over each naan bread to protect a little when cooking and place into the hot multi cooker on number 4 for 4 minutes on each side or until done.
7.Serve with curry, onion and tomato salad and mango chutney.

Pea and Ham Risotto

Ingredients
250g (10 oz) Arborio rice
1 large onion (chopped)
1 tsp mixed dried herbs
1 tbsp olive oil
150g (6 oz) cubed cooked ham
150g (6 oz) frozen peas
150g (6 oz) parmesan cheese (grated)
1.1 litre (1¾ pints) chicken stock
125ml (¼ pint) white wine
200g (8 oz) cream cheese
Salt and pepper
  Serves 6

Method
1.Place the onion and oil in the Multi-Cooker on number 3 and fry for 3 minutes.
2. Add the risotto rice and cook for 2 minutes stirring continuously.
3. Add the white wine, mixed herbs and stock, slowly stirring every 2 minutes with the lid on in-between. Cook for 12 minutes.
4. Add the peas, ham, cream cheese and remaining parmesan. Cook for a further 5 minutes stiring every couple of minutes. Season to taste.
5. Serve with grated parmesan and basil to garnish.

19

Red Lentil Soup

Ingredients

200g (7 oz) split red lentils
1 medium onion (finely chopped)
2 cloves garlic (finely chopped)
1 litre (1¾ pints) chicken or vegetable stock
2 tbsp olive oil
75g (3 oz) chorizo spicy sausage (thinly sliced)
50g 2 tbsp tomato puree
1 medium carrot (peeled and diced)
1 small red pepper (diced)
1 tbsp paprika

Garnish
Sour cream, parsley
     Serves 4

Method

1. Heat the olive oil in the Multi-Cooker at number 3½ then add the onion and garlic. Fry for 5 minutes without browning.

2. Add the paprika, red pepper, carrot, chorizo and tomato puree to the Multi-Cooker and cook for a further 3 minutes.

3. Add the lentils, stock and bring to the boil. Turn the multicooker down to 1 and place the lid on. Cook for 25 minutes, stirring every 4 minutes adding more water if necessary.

4. Finish with a spoonful of sour cream and garnish with parsley. Serve with crusty bread.

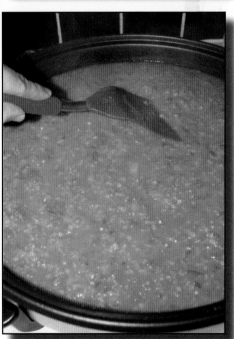

Salmon Pâté with Dill and Mustard Sauce

Ingredients

Pâté

2 small fillets of salmon
(approximately 150g or 6 oz each)
200g (8 oz) cream cheese
1 tbsp lemon juice
1 tbsp chopped parsley
100g (4 oz) cooked prawns
Salt & pepper

Dill Sauce

5 tbsp mayonnaise
2 tbsp chopped fresh dill
½ tbsp English mustard
1 tbsp vinegar
1 tbsp olive oil
     Serves 6

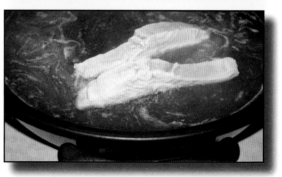

Method

1. Pour 1 litre (1 ¾ pints) of boiling water into the Multi-Cooker and place the salmon in the pan skin side down. Turn the Multi-Cooker to number 5.

2. Bring the water to the boil and then simmer on number 2 for 10 minutes or until cooked with the lid on.

3. Turn off the Multi-Cooker and place the salmon on a cold plate. Break up the salmon and allow to cool, then cover and chill in the fridge for two hours.

4. After two hours, flake the salmon into a large bowl (removing skin & bones) then add cream cheese, parsley, lemon juice and prawns.

5. Mix well and scoop into a quenelle (an oval or egg shape). Then place on a serving plate.

6. For the dill sauce simply mix together all the ingredients in a bowl and season to taste.

Drizzle or serve the dill sauce around the pate quenelles and serve with a garnish of a lemon wedge, along with fresh bread or toast.

Toasted Sandwich

Ingredients
8 bread slices
4 tbsp grated cheese
4 slices ham
50g (2oz) butter or margarine
50g (2oz) grilled peppers (optional)
Salt & pepper
        Serves 4

Method

1. Butter one side of each slice of bread.
2. Fill sandwiches with ham, cheese and peppers (or preferred filling) leaving the butter on the outside of the sandwiches.
3. Turn Multi-Cooker on number 3½.
4. Place sandwiches into the Multi-Cooker, butter side down.
5. Press down sandwiches with a strong spatula checking the cooking face regularly; turn over once brown and repeat the process for the other side.
6. Serve hot with a side salad.

25

Tomato and Basil Bruschetta

Ingredients
Topping
6 medium tomatoes (deseeded and diced)
1 small red onion (finely chopped)
12 basil leaves (torn finely)
3 tbsp olive oil
1 small clove garlic (finely chopped)
1 tbsp balsamic glaze
Salt and pepper
Base
1 stick French bread (sliced diagonally)
4 tbsp olive oil
1 clove garlic (finely chopped)
Garnish Basil leaves
     Serves 6

Method
1. Mix all topping ingredients in a bowl.
2. For the base, mix the olive oil with the garlic in another bowl.
3. Turn the Multi-Cooker to number 3½ and toast one side of the bread with the lid off for approximately 4 minutes. Brush the other side with the olive oil and garlic mixture and toast that side down for approximately 2 minutes.
4. Place all the toasted sliced bread on a plate then spoon the tomato and basil mixture on top and serve.

27

Wild Mushroom and Bacon Risotto

Ingredients

250g (10 oz) Arborio rice
1 large onion (chopped)
2 cloves garlic (finely chopped)
1 tsp mixed dried herbs
1 tbsp olive oil
25g (1 oz) butter
250g (10 oz) various mushrooms
(cleaned and sliced)
150g (6 oz) bacon (chopped)
50g (2 oz) parmesan cheese
(grated)
1.2 litre (2 pints) chicken stock
125ml (¼ pint) white wine
200g (8 oz) cream cheese
Salt and pepper
        Serves 4

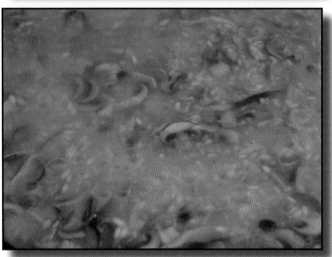

Method

1. Turn Multi-Cooker on to number 3½ and add the onion, oil, butter, bacon and mushrooms.
Fry for 3 minutes.
2. Add the risotto rice and cook out for 2 minutes, stirring all the time.
3. Add the white wine and the stock, slowly stirring every 2 minutes replace lid after stirring. Cook for 12 minutes.
4. Add the cream cheese and parmesan, gently mixing in for 3 minutes. Season to taste.
5. Serve with the fried mushrooms as a garnish along with parmesan shavings and a green side salad with French dressing.

29

Beef Bourguignon

Ingredients

1 kg (2lb 4 oz) stewing steak
100g (4 oz) streaky bacon (chopped)
1 carrot (peeled and sliced)
2 medium onions (sliced)
½ tsp salt
¼ tsp white pepper
2 tbsp plain flour
500ml (1 pint) red wine
250ml (½ pint) beef stock
2 tbsp tomato puree
1 garlic clove (finely chopped)
½ tsp mixed dried herbs
20 small button mushrooms (cleaned)
75g (3 oz) butter
1 tbsp olive oil
10 small shallots (peeled)
2 tbsp chopped fresh parsley
     Serves 6

Method

1. Turn on the Multi-Cooker to number 4½ and place the oil and butter in the pan. Fry the chopped bacon for two minutes then fry the beef until the outside starts to turn brown.
2. Add the sliced onions and shallots and fry for 2 minutes.
3. Add the carrots, garlic, salt, mushrooms, tomato puree and sugar.
4. Mix in the flour then add the wine, stock and mixed herbs. Stir and bring to the boil on number 5.
5. Turn down the Multi-Cooker to number 1 and simmer with the lid on for 1 hour, stirring every 7 minutes.
6. Garnish with the chopped parsley,serve with mashed potato and steamed vegetables.

31

Beef Stew and Dumplings

Ingredients
500g (approx 1lb 2oz) ground beef mince
1 large onion (chopped)
2 large carrots (chopped)
¼ swede (diced)
3 potatoes (peeled and diced)
1½ litres (2½ pints) beef stock
(made with 2 beef stock cubes)
3 rashers streaky bacon (chopped)
1 tbsp vegetable oil 1½ tbsp plain flour
½ tsp mixed dried herbs
1 tbsp soy sauce
1 parsnip (peeled and chopped)
Dumplings
200g (8 oz) self raising flour
100g (4 oz) suet
4 tbsp water
Garnish
Parsley
　　Serves 6

Method
1. Turn Multi-Cooker to number 3 and heat vegetable oil, add ground beef and fry until golden brown for about 5 minutes.
2. Add the onion and bacon and fry for 2 minutes.
3. Add the flour, stir for 1 minute, add the rest of the vegetables and herbs.
4. Slowly add the stock and bring to the boil.
5. Turn down to just under number 1 then add the soy sauce.
6. Simmer for 40 minutes, stirring every 10 minutes with the lid on.
7. Meanwhile mix the dumpling ingredients together and season, adding more water if needed to form a dough. Make into small balls ('ping pong' ball sized).
8. After 40 minutes bring the stew back to the boil then add the dumplings and cook for 20 minutes turning down to number 1, with lid on.

33

Calzone

Ingredients

Pizza dough
250g (10 oz) strong flour
100ml (4 fl oz) warm fresh milk (any type)
50ml (1½ fl oz) warm water (not boiled)
1 tsp dried yeast
2 tbsp olive oil
Pinch of salt
Filling
4 tbsp ketchup or tomato passata
50g (2 oz) cubed cheese
(cheddar, feta or mozzarella)
50g (2 oz) salami
6 cherry tomatoes (halved)
6 basil leaves
Pinch mixed dried herbs
        Serves 2 (cut in half)

Method

1. In a large bowl place the warm milk, water and dried yeast. Mix and leave for 5 minutes.
2. Add the flour and mix to form a dough. Knead for 5 minutes or use a food mixer with a dough hook, then knead in the olive oil.
3. Cover the bowl with a damp tea towel and leave in a warm place to rise for two hours.
4. Add the salt to the dough and knead into a large round circle to make calzone.
5. Fill with the tomato ketchup/passata then add the cheese, feta or mozzarella, salami, tomatoes, mixed herbs and basil leaves.
6. Brush milk around the edge of the dough circle and fold over like a pasty.
7. Flour both sides and place in the Multi-Cooker on number 3 with the lid on, cooking each each side for 4 minutes repeating the process again until cooked.
Serve with a side salad and cut the Calzone in half to make to make two individual portions.

Chicken Tikka Masala

Ingredients
200g (8 oz) raw chicken breast (cubed)
100g (4 oz) yogurt
2 tbsp barbecue tandoori seasoning
(double if you like it hot)
1 onion (finely chopped)
2 cloves of garlic (finely chopped)
½ tbsp grated ginger
1 tin 415g coconut milk
4 tbsp ground almonds
¼ tsp sugar
1 tin 295g condensed tomato soup
2 tbsp vegetable oil
300ml (½ pint) vegetable or chicken stock
2 tbsp sweet chilli sauce
1 tin chopped tomatoes
    Serves 6

Method
1. Mix the raw chicken with the yogurt, sugar and tandoori seasoning.
2. Turn the Multi-Cooker to number 3 then add the oil, ginger, garlic and onion to the pan. Fry for 2 minutes.
3. Add the marinated chicken and cook for 4 minutes, turning regularly.
4. Add the tomatoes, coconut milk, condensed tomato soup, stock, sweet chilli sauce and stir.
5. Bring to the boil then turn down and simmer on number 1 or just below 1 (for intermittent heat) for 20 minutes with lid on, stirring every 5 minutes.
6. After 20 minutes add the ground almonds and stir.
Serve with basmati or pilaf rice, naan bread, tomatoes and red onion salad with cumin seeds.

37

Chilli Beef Stir Fry

Ingredients
200g (6-8 oz) sirloin steak
(sliced into thin strips)
1 tbsp nut oil
1 tsp ginger (grated)
1 red chilli (finely chopped)
1 clove garlic (finely chopped)
1 tbsp soy sauce
½ tbsp vinegar
¼ tbsp sugar
1 tsp chinese five spice
1/4 tsp ground black pepper
50g (2 oz) mange tout
50g (2 oz) baby corn
1 red pepper (cut into strips)
1 yellow pepper (cut into strips)
50g (2 oz) mushrooms (sliced)
100g (4 oz) bean shoots
2 tbsp sweet chilli sauce
50ml (2 fl oz) chicken stock
½ tsp corn flour
          Serves 4

Method
1. Heat the Multi-Cooker for 1 minute on number 3.
2. Add the nut oil and sirloin strips to the Multi-Cooker and fry for 2 minutes.
3. Add the red chilli, ginger, garlic, soy sauce, vinegar, sugar, five spice and black pepper. Stir together and cook for a further 1 minute.
4. Stir in all the vegetables and keep stirring. Cook for 2 minutes.
5. Add the chicken stock and bring to the boil. Mix cornflower with a little water and Stir in and cook for 3 minutes on number 4 or until thickened.
6. Add the sweet chilli sauce and stir.
7. Serve with jasmine rice.

Chilli Con Carne with Tortillas and Mexican Chilli Cheese Dip

Ingredients

500g (1lb 2oz) minced/ground beef
1 large onion (finely chopped)
2 cloves garlic (chopped)
¼ tbsp chilli powder (more if you like it hot)
1 tin kidney beans in chilli sauce
1 tsp cayenne powder
2 tins tomatoes (chopped)
2 tbsp tomato puree
4 tbsp tomato ketchup
¼ ltr (½ pint) beef stock
1½ tbsp plain flour
3 medium fresh tomatoes (quartered)
8 mushrooms (washed and sliced)

Mexican chilli cheese dip
100ml (4 fl oz) sour cream
50g (2 oz) cheese with chilli (grated)
2 tbsp sweet chilli sauce
2 spring onions (finely chopped)
2 tbsp mayonnaise
　　Serves 6

Method

1. Place the beef into the Multi-Cooker on number 5, break up and fry with the onions and garlic.
2. Once the meat has browned, add the chilli powder and flour, mix well.
3. Add the kidney beans, cayenne powder, tinned tomatoes, tomato puree, tomato ketchup, fresh tomatoes and mushrooms. Stir again.
4. Add the beef stock and stir well then bring to the boil.
5. Turn down the heat to number 1 and replace the lid. Simmer for 20 minutes, stirring every five minutes then season and serve.
6. To make the chilli cheese dip, mix all the ingredients together in a bowl saving back a little cheese, spring onions and chilli sauce to garnish the top of the dip.

Handy Hints
To Make:-
Cornbread add 100g (4 oz) creamed sweet corn at stage 4 of the method and mix with the dough, then follow the rest of the recipe.
Corn Dogs make cornbread and add a hot dog to the middle of each dough ball, then follow the rest of the recipe .
Cheesy Dough bites place a cube of your favourite cheese in the middle of each dough ball and follow the rest of the recipe .
Serve with a tomato sauce dip mayonnaise and mustard.
To save time you can use a pre-bought packet of bread mix .
Amount displayed below is double the ingredient quantity.

Dough Bites / Cornbread / Corn Dogs

Ingredients

Dough

225g (8 oz) strong plain flour
or bread flour
½ tsp salt
1 tsp caster sugar
25g (1 oz) melted butter
150ml (¼ pint) lukewarm milk
13g (½ oz) fresh yeast

Filling variations

Hot dogs, creamed corn, cheese.
Serve with Chilli sauce, ketchup.
Serves 6

Method

1. Mix the yeast with the lukewarm milk and sugar and leave for 5 minutes.
2. Place the flour and salt into a bowl and mix in the melted butter.
3. Add the yeast liquid and mix for 5 minutes to form a soft dough.
4. Place the dough into a bowl and cover with a clean damp cloth and leave in a warm place for ten minutes.
5. Knead the dough for two minutes to reduce it to its original size.
6. Roll the dough into very small balls and dust with flour.
7. Set the Multi-Cooker to number 1½ and preheat with the lid on for two minutes with 1 tbsp water in the pan.
8. When the water has almost evaporated add the small balls and cook with the lid on for 10 minutes. Turn the balls every 3 minutes pressing down to flatten slightly to make bite size.

43

Duck in Orange Sauce

Ingredients
4 duck breasts
1 medium onion (chopped)
2 tbsp plain flour
250ml (8.5 fl oz) chicken stock
250ml (8.5 fl oz) orange juice
2 tbsp light brown sugar
2 oranges (peeled sliced and de-seeded)
1 tbsp sherry vinegar
2 tbsp orange liqueur
pinch of mixed dried herbs
        Serves 4

Method
1. Heat the Multi-Cooker to number 2, place the duck breasts in the pan skin side down and fry to protect the meat when cooking.
2. Cook for 10 minutes skin side down with the lid on.
3. Turn the breasts over then add

onions. Cook between 6 - 20 minutes on the other side. Remove the duck breasts when cooked to your personal preference. Place the duck breasts on a warm plate and cover.
5. Turn down the Multi-Cooker to number 1½ and add the flour to the onions. Stir well and mix in the orange juice (the juice will mix easier if warmed first), stock, mixed herbs, brown sugar, sherry vinegar and orange liquor.
6. Bring the sauce to the boil on number 5, stirring then turn to number 1 and simmer for 6 minutes with the lid off to reduce sauce.
7. Add the orange slices.
8. Return the duck to the pan and heat through. Serve with mashed potatoes and vegetables.

Gnocchi with Gorgonzola, Spinach and Pine Nuts

Ingredients
500g (1lb 2oz) ready made gnocchi
100g (4 oz) Gorgonzola or blue cheese
250ml white wine
250ml double cream
200g (2 oz) spinach (washed and dried)
75g (3 oz) pine nuts
1 tbsp olive oil
Salt and pepper to taste

Serves 4

Method
1. Toast the pine nuts in the Multi-Cooker on number 2 for two minutes with the oil until golden brown. Remove and set aside.
2. Add the Gorgonzola cheese to the Multi-Cooker and stir until it melts. Add the white wine and bring to the boil on number 5.

3. Turn the Multi-Cooker down to number 3 and add the double cream, stirring all the time.
4. Add the gnocchi and continue to stir for 2 minutes.
5. Turn the heat down to number 1 and stir until the sauce thickens.
6. Add the spinach, season with salt and pepper to taste, mixing well.
7. Serve with the toasted pine nuts as garnish

Handy Hint
Alternatively you can use Emmental or Gruyere cheese if you prefer. Leave out the spinach and add fried onions instead for a different texture. You can also add garlic salt to give some extra flavour.

47

Kedgeree

Ingredients
300g (12oz) long grain rice
350g (14oz) smoked haddock (fillet)
25g (1 oz) butter
1 large onion (chopped very finely)
1 tsp mild curry powder
4 tbsp double cream
4 hard boiled eggs (shelled and quartered)
2 tbsp chopped fresh parsley
(or 1 tbsp dried parsley)
Salt and pepper
      Serves 4

Method
1. Cook the the smoked haddock in the Multi-Cooker on number 2¼ for 6 minutes with the butter. Turn the heat down slightly if the fish starts to brown.
2. Place the cooked fish on to a plate and set aside, then fry the

onions in the juices and butter from the residue of the fish.
3. Add the rice to the onions and butter in the Multi-Cooker and fry for 2 minutes.
4. Add boiling water (approximately 850ml 1½ pints) and a pinch of salt and bring to the boil on 4, then cook with the lid on at number 2 for 15-20 minutes or until cooked, stirring every 4 minutes.
5. When the rice has cooked add the fish along with the cream, parsley and curry powder in the Multi-Cooker.
6. Replace the lid and cook on number 1 for a further 4 minutes.
7. Turn off and serve. Add two quarters of an egg to each portion.

49

Lamb Burgers

Ingredients
1 pack of minced lamb (makes 4 burgers)
1 onion (finely chopped)
1 tsp fresh rosemary
(or ½ tsp dried rosemary)
4 tsp redcurrant jelly
¼ tsp mint sauce
1 tbsp plain flour
Sesame seed buns
1 tbsp vegetable oil
        Serves 4

Method

1. Place minced lamb, onion, rosemary, redcurrant jelly, mint sauce and plain flour in a large bowl.
2. Mix all the ingredients together in the bowl by hand and make four burgers.
3. Add the oil to the Multi-Cooker and turn on to number 3 frying each burger for approximately 6 minutes on each side or until cooked.
5. Then place the burgers in the sesame seed buns .

Serve with salad, mayonnaise, relish or mustard.

Lemon Chicken

Ingredients

6 boneless chicken thighs (skinned)
2 tbsp light soy sauce
1 tbsp lemon juice
2 tbsp plum sauce

Covering

175g (7 oz) rice flour
¼ tsp garlic salt
¼ tsp Mixed herbs
Salt and pepper
7 tbsp vegetable oil to fry

Sauce

250ml (½ pint) boiling water
5 tbsp lemon juice
Zest of ½ lemon (then sliced)
¼ tbsp arrowroot
3 tbsp rice vinegar
1 tbsp plum sauce
        Serves 4

Method

. Place chicken in a bowl with the plum
sauce, lemon juice, light soy sauce and leave for ten minutes.
. Place rice flour, herbs and garlic salt in a bowl. Season and mix.
. Add oil for frying in the Multi-Cooker and heat at number 4½.
. Take chicken out of marinade and dip in the rice flour mixture piece-
y-piece place in Multi-Cooker. Cook each side for 5 minutes.
. Once cooked through, remove the chicken pieces and rest on a plate.
Add lemon juice to pan and turn down the heat to number 1.
. Stir round the lemon juice to de-glaze the pan then add the rice
inegar,boiling water, plum sauce, sugar and stir.
. Mix the arrowroot in a little cold water to form a runny paste and add
o the Multi-Cooker, stirring all the time.
. Add the chicken back to the Multi-Cooker and turn up the heat to
umber 3½ so the sauce is boiling. Add the sliced lemon, stir and serve
ith rice and steamed vegetables.

53

Mexican Style Rice

Ingredients
2 cups rice
2 chicken stock cubes
2-3 medium tomatoes (quartered)
2 cloves garlic
½ jalapeno pepper
1 tbsp olive oil
½ red onion chopped
4 cups of water
1 tsp cumin
    Serves 4

Method
1. Place the tomatoes, garlic, cumin, 1 chicken stock cube (crumbled), the red onion and jalapeno without seeds (or the entire jalapeno for spicier food) into a food processor. Blend until it is almost liquid but still has consistency (very small pieces). Set aside.

2. Heat the Multi-Cooker for 1 minute on number 2. Add the olive oil and fry the rice for 6-8 minutes or until golden.
3. Once golden, separate the rice and create a hole in the middle of the pan.
4. Pour the tomato mix into the centre of the rice and fry for 30 seconds. Stir the tomato mixture with the rice, continue to fry and stir for 2 minutes.
5. Add 4 cups of boiling water. Crumble a chicken stock cube into the Multi-Cooker. Bring to the boil and allow to boil for 2 minutes.
6. Turn the Multi-Cooker to setting 1 and cover.
7. Cook for approximately 15-20 minutes, then serve.

Paella

Ingredients
1 large onion (chopped)
2 tbsp olive oil
125g (5 oz) chorizo (cut into thin slices)
6 chicken thighs with skin
1 red pepper (diced)
1 tsp mixed herbs
2 cloves garlic (finely chopped)
200g (8 oz) paella rice
1 tsp paprika
1.2 litres (2 pints) chicken stock
A pinch of saffron strands (or ¼ tsp turmeric)
2 tbsp white wine vinegar
4 large tomatoes (de-seeded and diced)
3 tbsp frozen peas
Seafood
100g (4 oz) clams
100g (4 oz) mussels
100g (4 oz) squid in rings
100g (4 oz) raw shelled prawns
6 large unshelled tiger prawns
or pack of seafood mix
        Serves 6

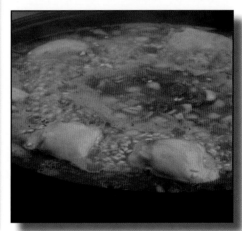

Method
1. Fry the chicken with the oil on number 4 with the lid on. Turn every couple of minutes for 5 minutes.
2. Add the chorizo, onions, garlic and red pepper and cook for a further 4 minutes with lid on. Stir every 2 minutes.
3. Add the rice and stir in. Turn down the heat to number 3 and slowly add the stock, saffron or turmeric, mixed herbs, white wine, vinegar and paprika. Cook for ten minutes with lid on.
4. Add all the seafood.
5. Cook for a further 7 minutes then add the peas and diced tomatoes. Cook for further 3 minutes with lid on, or until thoroughly cooked through.
6. Season, sprinkle with parsley and serve immediately.

Pasta with Ham and Parmesan

Ingredients
200g (8 oz) pasta twists
1 tbsp olive oil
1 stock cube
4 spring onions (chopped)
100g (4 oz) cubed ham
200ml (8 oz) crème fraîche
150g (6 oz) grated fresh parmesan
750ml (1 ½ pint) boiling water
10 cherry tomatoes (halved)
10 basil leaves
Pinch mixed herbs
Salt and pepper
Serves 4

Method
1. Turn on the Multi-Cooker and heat on setting 3½. Fry the spring onions in the olive oil for 1 minute.
2. Add the pasta, boiling water, stock cube and mixed herbs and boil with the lid on for 10-15 minutes at setting 3½ or until cooked.
3. Once the pasta is cooked the water should have reduced.
4. Mix in the ham, crème fraîche, parmesan and season to taste.
5. Garnish with basil leaves and cherry tomatoes.

Handy Hint
To make this dish more filling, dice the meat from a pre-cooked chicken and add with the ham.

Poached Trout with Herb Stuffing

Ingredients
2 trout (cleaned and gutted)
Stuffing
1 tbsp lemon juice
150g (6 oz) bread crumbs
1 tsp dried marjoram
1 tbsp chopped parsley
125 ml (¼ pint) white wine
500ml (1 pint) chicken or vegetable stock
25g (1 oz) butter
Sauce
25g (1 oz) very cold butter (cubed)
50ml (2 tbsp) double cream
King prawns to garnish
French beans for 2 people
1 courgette (chopped/cubed/sliced)
New potatoes for 2 people
1 carrot (peeled and sliced)
Serves 2

Method
1. Place the stock in the Multi-Cooker and turn to setting 3½.
2. Add the potatoes and cook for 12 minutes.
3. Add the French beans, carrots, courgette and cook out for 4 minutes.
4. Place the vegetables and potatoes into an insulated dish to serve later with the trout.
5. Mix all the stuffing ingredients together and place inside both trout.
6. Add the wine to the cooking stock in the Multi-Cooker and cook the trout and prawns on setting 3½ for 6 minutes on each side with the lid on.
7. Remove the fish and prawns from the Multi-Cooker and place on to a warm plate, covering with tin foil.
8. To make the sauce turn the Multi-Cooker to number 5 and reduce the remaining cooking liquid for 5 minutes, stirring all the time.
9. Add the cream and quickly stir in the cubed butter, seasoning to taste.
10. Serve the trout with the new potatoes, French beans, courgette, carrots and prawns then drizzle the sauce over the fish.

Pork Chops with Spicy Tomato Sauce with Stir-fry Cabbage

Ingredients

4 x pork steaks about 7mm (¼ inch) thick

Tomato coating for chops

4 tbsp tomato sauce

¼ tbsp honey

¼ tbsp cayenne pepper

½ tsp dark soy sauce

1 clove garlic (finely chopped)

½ tbsp olive oil

Cabbage Stir-fry

1 savoy cabbage (shredded)

2 cloves of finely chopped garlic

3 tbsp of vegetable oil

¼ tsp sesame seed oil

1 cm cube fresh ginger (finely chopped)

2 tsp dark soy sauce

Serve 4

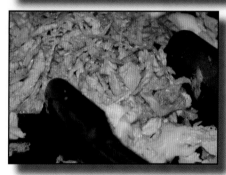

Method

1. Place oil and sesame seed oil in the Multi-Cooker and turn to number 4.
2. Add the garlic and ginger and fry for 1 minute.
3. Add the cabbage and fry for 5 minutes, leaving the lid on and stirring every 2 minutes.
4. Turn down the Multi-Cooker to number 2 and cook for 5 minutes, leaving the lid on and stirring every 2 minutes.
5. In a small bowl mix all the tomato coating ingredients together.
6. Place the cabbage into an insulated dish or warmed bowl, keep covered.
7. Place the pork chops in the Multi-Cooker at number 4 and start to brown.
8. Cook on each side for 2 minutes, then remove the chops, place onto a plate and with some paper towels dry both sides.
9. Place back in the pan and brush with the tomato coating, turning every 2 minutes and brushing with more tomato coating until it has all been used.
10. Once the chops are cooked, serve with the cabbage and a potato dish of your choice.

63

Pork Steaks with Wine and Apple Sauce

Ingredients
4 medium pork steaks
1 tbsp garlic paste
1 tbsp fresh sage (chopped)
(or ½ tbsp dried sage)
1 tbsp plain flour
150ml (¼ pint) medium white wine
225ml (8 fluid oz) vegetable stock
2 tbsp apple sauce
1 apple (peeled and chopped)
1 tsp olive oil
Salt and black pepper to taste
        Serves 4

Method
1. Heat the oil in the Multi-Cooker and add the chops. Cook for 3 to 4 minutes on each side.
2. Turn the Multi-Cooker to number 1. Cover chops with garlic and sage and fry for a further minute on each side.
6. Add oil then flour into the Multi-Cooker and gently stir for 30 seconds.
7. Slowly add the wine, stock, apple sauce, apples and bring to the boil.
8. Stir gently for 6 minutes with the lid off until the sauce has slightly thickened and season.

Serve with mash and steamed vegetables.

Quick Cheese Pasta

Ingredients
300g (12 oz) Penne pasta
750ml (1½ pints) boiling water
1½ stock cubes (chicken or vegetable)
160g (6 oz) grated cheese
4 tbsp (100g) cream cheese
3 rashers of bacon (chopped)
1 large onion (finely chopped)
1 clove garlic (finely chopped)
2 sliced tomatoes
1 ½ tbsp cornflour
5 tbsp milk
Pinch mixed dried herbs
Pinch sugar
Salt and pepper
Dressing
3 tbsp olive oil
½ tbsp French mustard
1 tbsp vinegar
Salt and pepper
Serves 4

Method
1. Fry bacon and onions for 5 minutes at number 4½, stirring continuously.
2. Add garlic and fry for a further 1 minute. Add boiling water and pasta.
3. Bring to the boil, add the stock cubes and mixed herbs then turn down Multi-Cooker to setting 1 and simmer for 15 minutes with the lid on.
4. Once the pasta is cooked add the milk, cream cheese, half the grated cheese, a pinch of sugar and mix well.
5. Mix the cornflour in a cup with a little water until it looks like cream and pour into the Multi-Cooker. Stir well and season to taste.
6. Stirring all the time, bring to the boil then turn off heat and add the rest of the cheese on top. Garnish with the sliced tomato and fresh pepper.
French Dressing
1. Place all ingredients in a bowl and mix with a hand whisk. Pour over the salad in a bowl and serve.

67

Red Thai Curry with Prawns and Aubergine

Ingredients

200g (8 oz) raw prawns
1 aubergine (cut into pieces)
3 tbsp picked coriander
1 onion (finely chopped)
2 cloves of garlic (finely chopped)
2 tbsp red Thai curry paste
1 tin coconut milk
2 tbsp lime juice
¼ tsp sugar
1 large carrot
(peeled and sliced diagonally)
100g (4 oz) spinach leaves
1 tbsp vegetable oil
150ml (¼ pint) vegetable
 or chicken stock
1 tbsp sweet chilli sauce
12 basil leaves
Serves 4

Method
1. Turn the Multi-Cooker to number 3½,
add the oil, onions and prawns. Cook for 3 minutes.
2. Add the aubergine soaked in lime juice, carrots, garlic and cook for a further 2 minutes.
3. Add the red Thai curry paste and stir. Cook for 1 minute.
4. Add the sugar, sweet chill sauce, stock and coconut milk. Simmer for 10 minutes on setting 1, stirring every few minutes with lid on.
5. Season to taste then add the spinach, coriander and stir thoroughly.
6. Garnish with the basil leaves, coriander and serve.

Handy Hint
Try using chicken instead of prawns.

69

Rösti Brunch

Ingredients
Rösti
3 large potatoes (peeled and grated)
1 large onion (peeled and grated)
1 egg
1 tbsp flour
Salt and pepper
Serve with bacon, eggs, sausages,
mushrooms, tomatoes.
Tomato ketchup or brown sauce
        Serves 4

Method
1. Dry grated potato and onion with paper towel and place in a bowl.
3. Mix in the egg and flour and season.
4. Turn on the Multi-Cooker to number 4½ and place in ½ tsp of oil.
5. Divide the mixture into 4 and place these into the Multi-Cooker. Press the mixture down with a strong spatula to form the shape of a pancake.
6. Cook for about 3 minutes on each side or until cooked thoroughly.
7. Remove the rösti from the pan and place on a plate with a sheet of greaseproof paper between each one. Keep in a warm oven at 100°C/200°F.
8. Cook the rest of the brunch in the Multi-Cooker to your taste and serve with the rösti. With the sausages I tend to cook them at number 3 for a few minutes first, making sure I turn them regularly. When they are almost ready I turn the Multi-Cooker down to number 2 and place the eggs in the centre of the pan with the lid on so that the heat builds up and cooks the top.

Sausages with Onion Gravy

Ingredients

1 pack sausages
2 onions (sliced)
1 tbsp vegetable oil
570ml (1 pint) instant gravy
1 glass red wine
1 tsp dark soy sauce
10 mushrooms (quartered)
1 tsp yeast extract (Marmite)
Pinch garlic salt
Salt and pepper
Serve with mashed potato and
steamed vegetables.
Serves 4

Method

1. Turn on the Multi-Cooker to number 3½ and add the sausages, onion and vegetable oil to the pan. Cook for 5 minutes, turning regularly until the onions start to colour.
2. Add the red wine, gravy, soy sauce, yeast extract and mushrooms.
3. Turn down the Multi-Cooker to number 1½ and cook with the lid on for 30 minutes, stirring every 4 minutes.
4. Season to taste and serve.

Handy Hint

Works well with pork fillet, sliced and fried or different types of sausage like wild boar.

Handy Hint
Add half of teaspoon of garlic granules and two
table spoons of dried stuffing mix to the coating for more flavour.
Great with a sweet chilli dip or mayonnaise dip. on a buffet.

Southern Fried Chicken

Ingredients
8 boneless and skinless chicken thighs
Marinade
150ml (¼ pint) sour cream
½ tsp celery salt
¼ tsp cayenne pepper
¼ tsp white pepper
¼ tsp cinnamon
Coating
6 tbsp plain flour
6 tbsp breadcrumbs
¼ tsp white pepper
¼ tsp cinnamon
¼ tsp paprika
¼ tsp celery salt
Oil for frying
Serves 4-6

Method
1. Mix all marinade ingredients and chicken together in a bowl.
2. In another bowl place all the coating ingredients and mix.
3. Place 8 tbsp of vegetable oil in Multi-Cooker on number 4.
4. Dip the marinated chicken in the coating ingredients until covered and place each piece carefully in the Multi-Cooker.
5. Cook the chicken for 12 minutes, turning every 2 minutes or until cooked
6. Remove the chicken pieces and place onto paper towel. Serve with corn bread, fries or mashed potato and gravy.

Spanish Omelette

Ingredients
1 tbsp olive oil
2 large Spanish onions (peeled and sliced)
4 large baking potatoes (peeled and cubed)
Omelette
9 medium eggs
30ml (1 oz) double cream
30ml (1 oz) milk
1 tbsp water
Variations
50g (2 oz) red pepper (diced)
50g (2 oz) chorizo sausage (diced)
50g (2 oz) tomato (deseeded & diced)
50g (2 oz) ham (diced)
     Serves 6

Method
1. Carefully pour 1 litre (1¾ pints) of boiling water into the Multi-Cooker and turn on to number 3½. Add the potatoes and boil for 5 minutes with the lid on.
2. Drain excess water off the potatoes and remove from the Multi-Cooker.
3. Add oil to the Multi-Cooker pan and fry onions at number 3½ for three minutes without burning them. Add the potatoes and Variations, fry on number 2 for a further 4 minutes.
4. Add all the omelette ingredients into a bowl and mix with a fork, then pour into the Multi-Cooker. Turn down Multi-Cooker to just under number 1 (so the thermostat light comes on / off) and cook out with the lid on for 12 minutes or until thoroughly cooked.
5. Using a plastic spatula cut into desired portions and turn over to show browned underside on the plate.

Special Fried Rice

Ingredients
900g (2lb) cooked long grain rice
2 medium eggs
1 tsp sesame seed oil
2 tsp dark soy sauce
50g (2 oz) frozen peas
50g (2 oz) cubed ham
100g (4 oz) raw prawns
50g (2 oz) red pepper (diced)
50g (2 oz) mushrooms (sliced)
4 spring onions (sliced diagonally)
    Serves 6

Method
1. Heat the sesame seed oil in Multi-Cooker on number 5, then add the prawns, spring onions, mushrooms. Stir and cook for 4 minutes or until the prawns are cooked.

2. Add the ham, peas, soy sauce, red pepper and stir.

3. Add the rice into the Multi-Cooker pan and stir and add soy sauce.

4. Whisk the 2 eggs in a bowl and pour into the centre of the rice and stir.

5. Place the lid back on and cook for 2 minutes at number 3 and serve.

Spicy Sausage Casserole

Ingredients
6 sausages or chorizo
2 red onions (sliced)
4 cloves garlic (finely chopped)
4 carrots (peeled & diced)
750g baby new potatoes (cubed)
10 mushrooms (sliced)
1 medium glass red wine
1 tbsp tomato puree
1 tsp smoked paprika
1½ tsp oregano
1 tin chopped tomatoes
1 tin condensed tomato soup
½ pt water
    Serve 4

Method
1. Put the sausages in the Multi-Cooker on number 3 and brown on each side for approximately 5 minutes.
2. Add the onion, garlic and oil to the pan and fry for 3 minutes, number 2.
3. Add the carrots, mushrooms and potatoes and turn to number 3, stirring every 2 minutes (lid on).
4. Add the tomato puree, stir and cook for 4 minutes, stirring every 2 minutes.
5. Add the red wine, paprika, oregano and salt and pepper. Simmer on number 2 for 3 minutes (lid on).
6. Add the chopped tomatoes and the tomato soup and water. Simmer at number 1 for 25 minutes, stirring every 10 minutes.

81

Steak with a Pepper Sauce

Ingredients
2 fillet steaks
(use sirloin or rib eye if preferred)
Timings are based on 1cm (½ inch) thick steaks.

Pepper Sauce
250ml (8.5 fl oz) double cream
1 tbsp fruity brown sauce or 1 tbsp
Worcestershire sauce with a ¼ tsp sugar
1 tbsp mayonnaise
1 tbsp brandy or sweet dessert wine (Marsala)
1 tbsp drained green pepper corns in brine
¼ tsp white or black pepper
1 onion (finely chopped)
25g (1 oz) butter
Vegtable oil for frying
        Serves2

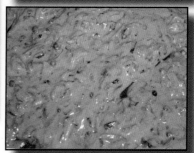

Method

1. Turn on the Multi-Cooker to number 5, allowing for the pan to heat up.
2. Place one of the steaks in the Multi-Cooker pan. Allow the heat to regain for a minute then place the other steak in the other side of the pan and leave for about 4 minutes or as long as you require. Do not move or turn the steak so that the meat has time to brown but not boil.
3. Turn the steaks over and add the onions and oil to the Multi-Cooker. Leave the steak for about 4 minutes on the other side, or to your taste.
4. Place the steak on a warm plate, cover to rest while you make the sauce.
5. In the Multi-Cooker add to the already fried onions the butter, green pepper corns and brandy. Allow the brandy to evaporate a little. Always remember to only pour in alcohol from a measured amount in a dish and never from a bottle for safety. Fry for 1 minute, then add the cream, fruity brown sauce, pepper and mayonnaise and give it a really good mix.
6. Add a couple of tbsps of boiling water if the sauce is getting too thick.
7. Give the sauce a good stir and serve over the steak along with salad and chips or jacket potatoes.

Teriyaki Prawns with Vegetable Stir Fry

Ingredients
250g (10 oz) king prawns (peeled)
2 cloves garlic (finely chopped)
1 large onion (diced)
½ tbsp ginger (peeled and finely chopped)
2 tbsp sweet chilli sauce
6 mushrooms (cleaned and quartered)
1 large carrot (peeled and slice diagonally)
100g (4 oz) mange tout
200g (8 oz) bean sprouts
2 tsp sesame seed oil
Salt and pepper
4 tbsp teriyaki sauce or mix
1 tbsp sake
½ tsp sugar
1 tsp dark soy sauce
¼ tsp miri
Serves 2 or 4 with rice

Method
1. Place the ginger, garlic, onion and sesame seed oil in the preheated Multi-Cooker at number 5. Stir fry ingredients for 2 minutes.
2. Add the prawns, carrots, bean sprouts, mushrooms and mange tout and stir. After 2 minutes turn down the heat to 3½ and cook for a further 3 minutes.
4. Add the teriyaki and sweet chilli sauces and stir for a further 2 minutes.
5. Serve with steamed sticky rice and steamed pak choi.

Handy Hint
Add sweet chilli sauce to spice it up. Alternatively use chicken instead of prawns, and as a different flavour just add a tbsp of hoisin sauce.

85

Tomato and Mince Pasta Bake

Ingredients
500g (1lb 2oz) ground/minced beef
3 rashers bacon (chopped)
6 mushrooms (sliced)
1 large onion (chopped)
2 cloves garlic (finely chopped)
2 tbsp tomato purée
2 tbsp tomato ketchup
1 chicken stock cube
1 400g tin chopped tomatoes
1½ litres (3 pints) boiling water
300g (12 oz) dried pasta shells
150g (6 oz) sliced and torn mozzarella
Pinch mixed herbs
Garnish
Basil leaves
      Serves 6

Method
1. Turn the Multi-Cooker on to number 4 and add the mince. Fry for 3 minutes.
2. Add the bacon, onions, garlic, mushrooms and tomato purée and cook for a further 3 minutes, stirring regularly.
3. Add 1½ litres (3 pints) of boiling water to the pan along with the dried pasta, stock cube and mixed herbs and put the lid on. Bring to boil then turn down to setting 2 and cook for 10 minutes, stirring every 3 minutes.
4. Turn up the heat to number 5, then add the chopped tomatoes, tomato ketchup and season with salt and pepper. Stir every minute with the lid off and mix well for 5 minutes.
5. Turn the Multi-Cooker off and then add the torn mozzarella cheese and garnish with the basil leaves.

Tuna Pasta

Ingredients
1 can condensed mushroom soup
175g (6 oz) tinned tuna (drained)
50g (2 oz) frozen peas
50g (2 oz) tinned sweetcorn (drained)
225g (8 oz) Vermicelli pasta
275ml (½ pint) cold water
Salt and pepper

Garnish
French bread
Salad
      Serves 4

Method
1. Empty the can of soup into the Multi-Cooker.
2. Add the pasta.
3. Add the water and stir.
4. Cook on number 3 for 5 minutes.
5. Reduce heat to number 1 and add the tuna, peas, sweetcorn and salt.
6. Replace the lid and cook for a further 12 minutes.
7. Stir and leave to stand for 1 minute before serving.

Veggie Burger

Ingredients
1 small onion (finely chopped)
1 clove garlic (crushed)
2 carrots (peeled and grated)
1 small courgette (grated)
75g (3 oz) cheese (grated)
1 tbsp soy sauce
200g (8 oz) mashed potato
50g (2 oz) sweetcorn
50g (2 oz) frozen peas
1 medium egg
200g (8 oz) plain flour (+ extra for rolling)
1 tbsp olive oil (+ extra for frying the burgers)
Pinch of mixed herbs
        Serves 4-8

Serve with potato salad, green salad, relish.

Method
1. Place the olive oil in the Multi-Cooker at number 3½, then fry the onions and garlic for 3 minutes.
2. Add the courgette, carrots, sweetcorn, frozen peas and mixed herbs, cook for 3 minutes.
3. Place the mashed potato in a large bowl and add the contents of the Multi-Cooker to the bowl. Then add the flour, soy sauce, egg and mix together.
4. Form into small burgers, coat in the flour and place on plate.
5. Chill the burgers in the fridge for an hour so that they are set and easier to fry. (They can be frozen at this stage for a later date)
6. Turn the Multi-Cooker to number 3½ and add oil for frying.
7. Place the veggi burgers into the Multi-Cooker and fry on each side for 5 minutes, turning carefully (longer if frozen)
8. Serve in a burger bun with salad, onion, mayonnaise and sliced tomato.

Apple Crumble

Ingredients
220g (8 oz) plain flour
1 tbsp grated lemon rind
Pinch of salt
150g (5 oz) butter
50g (2 oz) soft light brown sugar
10 cooking apples
(peeled, cored and chopped into cubes)
1 tbsp golden syrup
     Serves 6-8

Method
1. Place 25g (1 oz) of the butter into the Multi-Cooker on number 1 and add the chopped apple. Cook gently for 10 minutes.
2. Mix together the butter,flour, salt, and brown sugar in a large bowl, rubbing until the mixture resembles breadcrumbs (this can be done in a food processor)
3. When the apples are tender, pour over the golden syrup and roughly sprinkle over the crumble mix.
4. Cover and cook for a further 10 minutes. .

Handy Hint
You can replace the apples with any similar fruit, e.g. pears, berries, rhubarb. If you want more flavour add a couple of drops of a fruit liqueur. Serve with whipping cream or crème fraiche.

93

Banana Cake with Chocolate Caramel

Ingredients
Cake mix
100g (4 oz) self raising flour
100g (4 oz) butter (at room temperature)
100g (4 oz) light brown caster sugar
2 medium eggs (at room temperature)
2 ripe banana
Flavouring
2 chocolate caramel bars
(cut into thin slices)
125ml (¼ pint) double cream
          Serves 6

Method
1. Grease six ramekins with butter.
2. Distribute caramel pieces equally between the bases of each ramekin and add a tablespoon of cream.
3. Mix all the cake ingredients together in a large bowl.
4. Add the sliced bananas into the mixture.
5. Place 2 large tbsp of the cake mixture into each ramekin.
6. Place the ramekins into Multi-Cooker.
7. Place 2 litres (3½ pints) of boiling water into the Multi-Cooker on number 4½.
8. Boil for 25 minutes or until cooked. (place a knife into the pudding and if it comes out clean the pudding is ready)
9. Serve with thick cream, a sprig of mint and fresh raspberries.

95

Chocolate Croissant Pudding

Ingredients
12 croissants
150g 6 oz chocolate spread
(I use the one made of nuts)
150ml 6 floz double cream
410 ml 3/4 pt whole milk
125g 5oz dark brown sugar
5 medium eggs
75g 3oz drinking chocolate
or cocoa powder
        Serves 6-12

Method
1. Slice all the croissants in half and spread with chocolate spread.
2. Place the chocolate croissants into the Multi-Cooker.
3. Place the cocoa powder or drinking chocolate into large bowl and mix with a little of the milk to form a paste. Then add the rest of the milk whisking all the time.
4. Add cream, sugar and eggs and mix well.
5. Use a large sieve that you would use for flour and sieve the liquid over the croissants to remove any lumps and also break up the albumen in the eggs.
6. Allow to soak for 30 minutes to absorb the chocolate custard mix.
7. Turn on Multi-Cooker on number 3 for 6 minutes then just down to number 1 for 14 minutes. Serve the chocolate custard once it has set to your taste.

Chocolate Orange Puddings

Ingredients
Cake mix
100g (4 oz) self raising flour
100g (4 oz) butter or margarine
(at room temperature)
2 eggs medium (at room temperature)
100g (4 oz) soft brown sugar
¼ tsp vanilla extract
100g (4 oz) cocoa powder
100g (4 oz) chocolate chips
2 tbsp orange liqueur
Orange flavoured chocolate
Base
Golden syrup
2 tbsp orange liqueur
1 Orange peeled and segmented
To serve
100g (4 oz) double cream
Grated chocolate
Serves 6

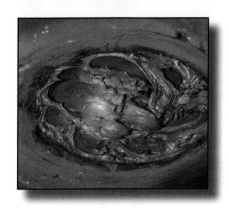

Method
1. Mix the chocolate cake mixture ingredients together in a large bowl.
2. Mix together the golden syrup, orange segments and orange liqueur from the base ingredients and divide into the six ramekins.
3. Divide the chocolate cake mixture into the six ramekins on top of the golden syrup mix.
4. Place a piece of orange flavoured chocolate in the centre of the cake mix of each ramekin.
5. Place 2 litres (3½ pts) of boiling water into Multi-Cooker at number 3½.
6. Place the ramekins into the Multi-Cooker. Place a dessert spoon in the base of the Multi-Cooker with the handle resting on the rim and place the lid on top, **reference page 114.** Boil for 20 minutes adding more liquid if necessary.(To check if cooked thoroughly, place a knife into the pudding, if it comes out clean the pudding is done.)
7. Serve each pudding with a drizzle of double cream, chocolate and a real orange segment soaked in orange liqueur.

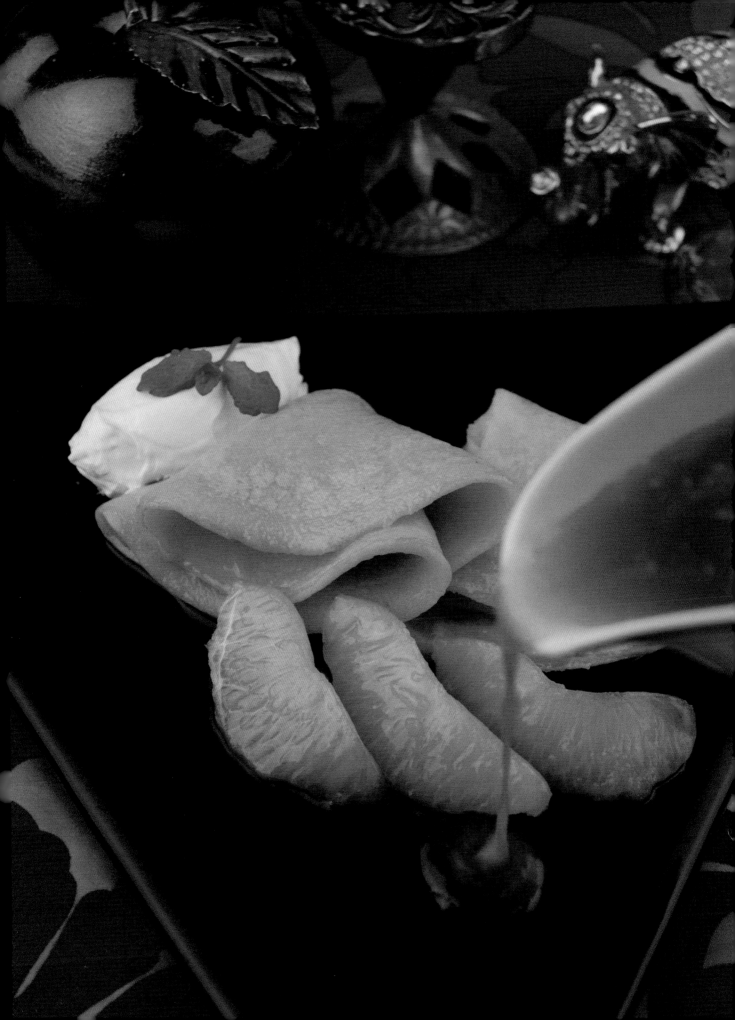

Crêpe Suzette

Ingredients
Pancake mix
250g (10 oz) plain flour
2 medium eggs
500ml (18 fl oz) milk
50g (2 oz) caster sugar
50g (2 oz) butter
Pinch of salt
Filling
2 oranges (peeled, segmented)
8 tbsp orange liqueur
3 tbsp golden syrup
50g (2 oz) butter
125ml (¼ pint) fresh orange juice
Serves 6

Method
1. Place flour in a bowl. Add sugar and slowly whisk the milk and eggs into the mixture. Add a pinch of salt. Whisk well until the mixture is lump free.
2. Place butter from pancake mix ingredients into Multi-Cooker on number 4½. When it starts to brown turn off and then add the browned butter to the pancake mix.
3. Heat Multi-Cooker to number 3. When the pan is hot add a ladle full of the pancake mix and allow to set, then flip the pancake over.
4. Remove the pancake and set aside on some greaseproof paper then repeat the process 11 times or until all the pancake mix is finished.
5. Place the butter from the filling ingredients into the Multi-Cooker on number 4, add the orange juice, golden syrup, orange liquor to the pan and bring to the boil. Add the orange slices.
6. Place pancakes into the Multi-Cooker and heat in orange juice mixture, folding each pancake in half and then into quarters.
7. Serve with double cream and a sprig of mint.

Dropped Scones

Ingredients
175g (6 oz) plain flour
¼ teaspoon salt
1½ teaspoons baking powder
50g (2 oz) rolled oats
75g (3 oz) butter (chilled and cubed)
1 egg (beaten)
275ml (½ pint) milk
Serves 6

Method
1. Place the flour, salt, baking powder and oats into a mixing bowl.
2. Rub in 50g (2 oz) of butter until the mixture has the consistency of breadcrumbs.
3. Stir in the egg and the milk and mix together with a wooden spoon until blended.
4. Cover with cling film for 15 minutes.
5. After 15 minutes heat the Multi-Cooker to number 3 and add the remaining butter. Turn down the heat to number 2.

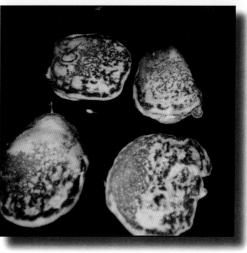

6. Once the butter has melted, simply take a tablespoon of the scone mixture and drop the spoonful into the Multi-Cooker.
7. Repeat until mixture is all used.
8. Cook for 2 minutes each side or until the scones are golden brown.

Handy Hint
These little scones make a lovely treat and there are so many variations. You can add 50g (2 oz) of any of your favourite dried fruit to the above mixture, you can serve with cold berries of your choice and crème fraiche. A nice alternative is to pour chocolate sauce on the hot scones and finish with whipped cream and flaked almonds.

Raspberry & Coconut Pudding

Ingredients
Coconut Cake
100g (4 oz) butter (at room temperature)
100g (4 oz) self raising flour
100g (4 oz) caster sugar
2 medium eggs (at room temperature)
100g (4 oz) desiccated coconut
100g (4 oz) ground almonds
Base
6 tbsp raspberry jam
Extra butter (for greasing the ramekins)
2 tbsp dessicated coconut
(for dusting ramekins)
Serves 4

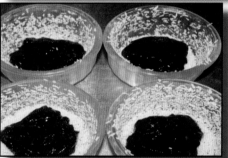

Method
1. Grease only the inside sides of the
ramekin dishes being careful to avoid the base. Sprinkle the desiccated coconut into the ramekins over a large bowl and turn them round so that the coconut sticks to the edge of the ramekin.
2. Divide the jam into the base of the ramekins.
3. Mix all the coconut cake ingredients together in a bowl to make the cake mix.
4. Place 2 heaped tablespoons of the cake mix in each of the ramekins.
5. Pour 2 litres (3½ pints) of boiling water into the Multi-Cooker and turn on to number 5.
6. Place each ramekin into the water and steam for 25 minutes or until cooked. Place a knife into the pudding, if it comes out clean then the pudding is cooked.
7. Place a spoon halfway into the pan to avoid the lid rattling when boiling, **reference page 114** (the handle may become so take care when handling).
8. Turn out and serve with custard or cream.

Rice Pudding with Apricots

Ingredients
330g (13 oz) pudding rice
2 tins evaporated milk
(approx 410g or 14½ oz each)
2 pints of whole milk
50g (2 oz) caster sugar
75g (3 oz) light brown sugar
¼ tsp ground nutmeg
12 whole dried apricots (in quarters)
75g (3 oz) butter
Apricot puree
2 tbsp apricot jam
1 tin apricots (drained)
1 tbsp icing sugar
　　　Serves 6

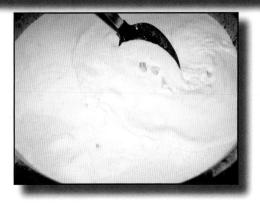

Handy Hint

Method

1. Place all ingredients into Multi-Cooker on setting 4½ and bring to the boil, stirring occasionally.
2. Once at boiling point turn down the heat to setting 1 and cook for 20 minutes, stirring every 3 minutes.
3. For the apricot puree place all the ingredients into a food processor and blend well.
4. Serve the rice pudding on a plate with the apricot around the edge. Garnish with a sprig of mint.

Spicy Prunes

Ingredients
450g (1 lb) large fresh prunes
(de-stoned)
150ml (¼ pint) rum
150ml (¼ pint) red wine vinegar
200g (8 oz) dark brown sugar
1 cinnamon stick
Juice and zest of 1 lemon
Juice and zest of 1 orange
Serve with
Ice cream, sprig of mint
and cinnamon stick

Serves 4

Method
1. Soak the prunes in the rum, vinegar, juice of lemon and orange for an hour.
2. Cook the prunes in the Multi-Cooker with all the liquid and bring to the boil on number 4.
3. Cover, turn Multi-Cooker down to number 2 and simmer for 4 minutes.

4. Add the sugar, zest of the lemon and orange and the cinnamon stick and simmer gently for another 4 minutes. Serve with ice cream.

Handy Hint
The texture of the hot prunes and cold ice cream is sensational .
You can add dried apricots to the prunes for a different flavour.

Syrup Puddings

Ingredients
Cake Mix
100g (4 oz) self raising flour
100g (4 oz) butter or margarine
100g (4 oz) caster sugar
2 medium eggs (at room temp)
½ tsp vanilla essence
Base
4 tbsp golden syrup
Fillings
25g (1 oz) chopped glacé cherries (per ramekin)
25g (1 oz) sultanas (per ramekin)
25g (1 oz) chopped apricots (per ramekin)
25g (1 oz) pecan nuts (per ramekin)
Serves 6

Method
1. Mix cake mixture ingredients together in a large bowl.
2. Grease 6 ramekins and divide the golden syrup into the bases of each (along with your chosen filling if using one).
3. Divide the cake mix between the ramekins.
4. Place 2 litres (3½ pints) of boiling water into the Multi-Cooker and turn on to setting 3½.
5. Very carefully place the ramekins into the Multi-Cooker. Place a dessert spoon in the base of the Multi-Cooker with the handle resting on the rim and place the lid on top, **reference page 118.** Boil for 20 minutes adding more liquid if necessary. To check if cooked thoroughly, place a knife into the pudding, if it comes out clean the pudding is done. The spoon handle will be hot, so handle with care.
6. Serve with custard or cream

Handy Hint
Great served with fresh blueberries or raspberries. Can be served with crème fraiche.

Winter Warming Fruit Salad

Ingredients
110g (4 oz) caster sugar
1 tbsp lemon juice / squeeze ½ lemon
3 tbsp orange liqueur
2 sprigs of mint
2 oranges (peeled and quartered)
400g (14 oz) strawberries (halved)
1 pear (peeled and cut into slices)
110g (4 oz) white grapes (washed)
110g (4oz) black grapes (washed)
100ml (¼ pint) water
     Serves 6

Method

1. Place all liquid ingredients (water, alcohol and fruit juices) into the Multi-Cooker on number 3 with the sugar and stir until the sugar dissolves.
2. Gently simmer for 2 minutes.
3. Add all the fruit.
4. Stir gently, cover and simmer for 5 minutes on number 1.
5. Serve and garnish with the sprigs of mint.

Handy Hint
Serve immediately with either double cream or crème fraiche. If you wish you can add any fruit of your choice and if you don't wish to use an orange liquor you can use any fruit based liqueur. If you want to go nuts, just add some chopped mixed nuts on top of the fruit mixture before you serve.

Mouth-wateringly delicious!

Handy Hint To Let Steam Escape

There is a vent in the lid of the Multi-Cooker which allows steam to escape during cooking. This is fine for simmering, however, when boiling place a spoon between the lid and the edge of the Multi-Cooker to let any excess steam escape. When handling the spoon always use an oven mitt / cloth.

Rough Guide To Cooking

Settings

No. 0-1 Warm – This is great for keeping things warm, especially for a buf when you want to maintain the temperature but not continue to cooking.

No. 2 - Slow Cook – This is for cooking meats slowly, tenderizing over tim

No. 3 - Saute/ Grill – Medium heat suitable cooking thicker foods such as potatoes, browning on the outside and still cooking all the way through.

No. 4 - Roast – A heat for cooking meats slower than frying. Great for cooking meats in gravy's and stocks.

No. 5 - Flash Fry – Is for fast, high heat cooking, great for steaks, chops and stir-fry's.

Square Cooker

When using a square cooker tempretures may vary so please adjust accordinly.

If you have any questions regarding the

recipes within this book, please feel free to write to us at:

Email us on: cook@paulbrodel.co.uk